Bringing Home Your Puppy

Leslie Oakley

Photographs by: Leslie Oakley and Dawg
Gone Photography

DEDICATION

To my fiancé Dave for giving me the confidence to write, to my parents Dan and Kelli for always telling me I could do anything I put my mind to, and to Hercules (RIP) who put me through so much, I had to buckle down and learn everything I could about animal behavior to keep our family whole.

CONTENTS

ACKNOWLEDGMENTS

I have a small family, but everyone in it has in some way helped to form me into the woman that I am. My love and joy for animals has always been nurtured and supported from my childhood to adulthood. I thank my parents Dan and Kelli Oakley for always supporting me with my passion for animals and for loving me for who I have always been. I also want to thank my fiancé Dave for supporting me to do whatever makes me happy and for believing in me to succeed.

1 PREPARE

There are so many joys that come with bringing in a new puppy to your home and life. The love you feel for the innocent, playful and adorable bundle will grow day by day and become a strong bond between you and your new loved family companion. Just like bringing a child into the world, you need to be ready. There are a lot of household dangers that can harm your new puppy; some you may never have thought could be harmful.

Preparation is key to protecting your new puppy. Puppies usually come home with their new owners between 8 and 10 weeks of age. A good breeder will have sent your puppy home with medical paperwork proving that the puppy has been given, and is up to date on, vaccinations. However, even if the puppy has had 2 sets of shots, he is NOT fully protected from disease. The young puppies will still be very susceptible to what they encounter. That is why it is important to rid your home of potential threats BEFORE the puppy comes home from the breeder. This includes but is not limited to, cleaning your floors (with bleach if possible but if not an antibacterial will do). You should vacuum any carpeted area and step in diluted bleach while wearing your shoes to kill any harmful germs that have accumulated (those germs will spread right back to your clean floors if this step is not done). I do realize you cannot keep every germ out of your house... However, there are ways to limit them. If you have a backyard or a patio that you plan to allow your puppy to explore, I would take similar steps. The concrete can be bleached down and any old dog toys from previous dogs should be thrown away or thoroughly cleaned with bleach. While you are outside cleaning your yard, keep an eye out for other harmful objects, such as pieces of glass, nails sticking out of wood fences, poisonous plants (research different sites online to compile a list), and anything small enough for the puppy to put in his mouth and swallow (this could lead from an upset stomach to a major surgery for intestinal blockage).

Do you have an older dog at home, waiting for his puppy companion to come home? If so, that is great! I think puppies thrive when they have a companion to help them grow and learn their family's routines. However, having another dog at home prior to the puppy's arrival can also be harmful. How active is your current dog? Do you walk the dog? Go to dog parks? How about trips to the pet store for treats and toys? All of these activities are very fun for your dog, but very dangerous to do before bringing in a new puppy. Pet stores, dog parks and walks can bring disease into your home without you knowing it. A dog owner who loves their dog will make sure the dog got his vaccinations when needed as that dog grew up. Throughout the dog's life, just as children do, the dog has built up a better immune system, allowing your dog to go on adventures, be exposed to disease and never get sick. However, your dog being exposed to these diseases do bring them into your home. The disease can travel through their saliva and their hair (specifically on their paws from the different places they visit). This is why it is important to change your routine a couple weeks prior to bringing home a new puppy. Give your current dog a good bath, scrubbing the bottom of his paws. After the bath, keep the dog home, or at least away from any areas where other dogs frequently go. This will limit the disease from coming into your home prior to bringing in a new puppy, thus, allowing your new puppy to come home to a safe environment.

Now are you ready to bring that cute fur ball home? Not yet. It would be a good idea to have all the puppy supplies you will need to care for the puppy, at home first. A crate, for housebreaking if you choose to use one, food and water bowls that are size appropriate, puppy pads (if you plan to train your puppy to use them), puppy food (not dog food – there is a difference), a bed or blanket for his sleeping area, a brush (if you purchased a puppy who will require grooming), and chew toys for your teething puppy. Now, once you have prepared your home, you are ready to bring your puppy home.

2 THE DAY HAS COME

The day to pick up your new family addition has finally come. He is going to be picked up and driven back to your warm and cozy environment, that to you, is extremely stress free and comfortable. As exciting as this day is to you, please remember, this can be a stressful day for your new puppy.

Your new puppy is going to be taken away from his mother, his siblings, and his owners (your breeder) for the very first time in his life. This can be stressful for your new puppy. He can be a little more reserved during this period, while he adjusts to the new living arrangements. The adjustment period can be as short as a few minutes and last up to a couple days. Every puppy will react to situations differently. It can help to bring a towel with you when you pick up your puppy from the breeder, so that you could rub the mom of the puppies down and / or the other puppies. This gives you something to take home and place in the puppy's sleeping area that has a familiar smell for him. Some breeders automatically send something home with the puppy for that very reason.

Before you leave the breeder's home with your new puppy, make sure you were given all the information needed. You should, at a minimum, get paperwork showing the puppy's deworming schedule and the vaccinations he has been given. Don't leave without this paperwork. Any vet you choose for your new puppy will want to see his medical records given to you by the breeder.

Now you are ready to bring your puppy home. If you are traveling alone, bring a crate or kennel for the puppy to be placed in during your drive home. Driving alone with a loose puppy in the car can cause distractions, among other things. It is simply safer for the puppy to be confined for the drive. However, if you have a passenger with you, you have the option of allowing them to handle and control the puppy, while you drive the vehicle. Bring a towel for your passenger to hold the puppy in. The towel can be used while holding the puppy and can come in handy if the puppy gets a bit nervous or car sick. For long car rides, depending on the time of your pick up, you could ask the breeder to keep any food away from the puppy for a couple hours prior to departure. It could help him to not get an upset stomach on the drive home that could cause him to vomit.

Once your puppy is home, take him to your designated puppy area. This is an area you have set up and made safe for the puppy to freely roam and play. The puppy should not immediately have full run of the house. This can cause confusion and it is usually very hard to fully "puppy proof" your whole house. By giving the puppy a designated area, he can feel confident while roaming and playing and you can rest assured the puppy and your home are safe. This can also help with house breaking your puppy. The smaller the area he has in the beginning, the easier it is for him to recognize it is not the appropriate potty area (with your help, of course).

During the day, the puppy should always have access to fresh, clean water. I have found that keeping the water in heavier dishes works best, to keep him from accidently knocking it over and causing the water to spill on the floor. Along with water, the puppy should have some chew toys that he can chew on throughout the day and bedding to rest on (whether it is in a crate or just set up on the floor).

3 INTRODUCING YOUR PUPPY TO YOUR CURRENT FAMILY PETS

A lot of puppy owners, being the animal loving people that most of them are, already have an adult dog at home and are bringing in a new puppy as both a companion to them and to their current pet. This can be such a blessing to a new puppy, going into a home where the puppy has an immediate playmate and companion aside from his new owners. However, not all dogs are pleased with the idea of having a puppy in their home. For this reason, we have a special way of introducing your new puppy to your current dog. If you have been visiting your new puppy at the breeder's home prior to the puppy's departure, bring a towel with you and rub the puppy down while you hold him so the towel is covered in the new puppy's scent. This towel can then be brought back home with you, days or even weeks before the puppy turns 8 weeks old and is available to come home with you. Set up your new puppy's crate and leave the door open, with the towel that you used to get the puppy's scent placed inside the crate as the bedding. Allow your current dog to put his head into the crate to smell the new scent and adjust to it prior to bringing the puppy into your home.

Once it is time to bring your new puppy home, remind yourself that not only is this day going to be stressful on the new puppy, but it is also going to be stressful on your current dog. Once you are home with the new puppy, carefully place him in a safe area where he can run around but is not free to roam with your current dog. It is best if there is a barrier between them such as a baby gate or a puppy pen so the two of them can smell each other and see each other, but yet they are still completely separate. I always remind the new owners of our puppies who have current dogs that it is very important that your current dog feel loved just as much now as he did before, or if not, more than he did before the puppy arrived. Focus more attention to your current dog than you do to your new puppy (without ignoring the puppy). You want this new addition to feel exciting and joyful to your current dog. More attention from his owners will make him associate the new addition to positive attention.

I do stress to owners that sometimes it is in the puppy's best interest to be crated or separated from the current dog for the first few days when nobody is home to monitor their play time. This is for a couple reasons. The current dog is older, usually bigger, and can be more forceful or dominant during the play time with his new companion. Sometimes our current dogs do not realize that the puppy is more fragile and cannot handle the rough play yet. There is also going to be a "pecking" order between the two of them. One will win the dominant role, and if it is going to be the current dog (which is normal), he can be a little more forceful in establishing his dominance over the puppy. Usually this does not physically hurt the puppy. It is more of an understanding between the two of them of who gets to be in charge. While the dog and puppy are adjusting to their new status, it is just safer for both dogs to be monitored when together until you, the owner, can safely say that they can live together peacefully.

Now, introducing a new puppy to a cat is slightly different. Cats, being a whole different type of species, react differently than dogs. Their personalities range all across the board, so there is no right or wrong way to introduce the puppy. In my experience, for cats that are not as social, it seems to help to put the cat in a bedroom and allow the puppy and the cat to smell each other under the doorway. The door is a good barrier to keep the cat safe from puppy trampling, but allowing him to get close enough to the puppy for a good smell. For cats that seem to adjust a little quicker and accept change easier, this can be accomplished through a crate or a baby gate separating the 2 rooms. The cat would be able to go in and out of the rooms, but the puppy would be held back by the gate. This way, when the cat has had enough of the puppy, the cat can "escape". Either way you choose, I would make it a priority that the cat has a safety zone the puppy cannot get into. This does not need to be a permanent change. Just long enough for the 2 companions to adjust to their new living situation together.

4 HOW MUCH TO FEED YOUR PUPPY

Feeding your puppy a good diet is ideal, just as you would a child. The first thing to remember is that puppies need "puppy" food (not dog food). There is a difference in the nutritional value and ingredients in dog food vs. puppy food. Hopefully, your breeder has told you what food your puppy was on at the breeder's home and you were able to buy a bag of the exact same food. You do not need to keep the puppy on the food he was fed at the breeder's home; however, it is a very good idea to buy a bag of it and mix the food the puppy is used to with the food you want to switch the puppy to. Start with 3 parts of the food the puppy is used to and add 1 part of the food you want the puppy to eventually end up eating. Using a good 2 weeks or more, slowly change the portions from being mostly the original food to half the original food and half the new food. Once you have that accomplished and your puppy is still eating normally and acting healthy, start to make the food mixture 3 parts of the new food to 1 part of the old food that was used by the breeder. Eventually, over time, you will have slowly stopped putting in any of the original food and are only filling the bowl with the food you want him to eat. It does take time, so be patient. This is the best way for your puppy to adjust to a new food.

Puppies are constantly growing. They need nutrition to keep their bodies healthy and growing at the appropriate rate. When you first bring a puppy home, it is ideal if you are able to feed the puppy three times a day (morning, afternoon, and early evening). Put a bowl of food down in the morning and give the puppy 15 minutes to eat as much food as he wishes. (The puppy will not over eat so you do not need to worry about the amount of food he eats at this age). Once he finishes his breakfast, pick up the bowl of food and take the puppy out to go potty. (Immediately after eating his meal, your puppy will need to go outside to go potty). Repeat this step for lunch and dinner. The puppy will learn that his food gets put down for a limited time and picked back up. This will teach him to eat when the food is in his bowl, which puts him on a feeding schedule. A feeding schedule is important with a puppy because it will spread the income of nutrition into the puppy during the day, helping to keep him full of energy and to make sure he does not go hungry throughout the day. This is especially important with the extra small breeds that are under 6lbs. Their sugar levels can drop quickly and they can become seriously ill if they do not get a sugar income throughout the day.

A bonus to putting your puppy on a feeding schedule is that you are also putting the puppy on a potty schedule. Every time the puppy eats a meal, he needs to be taken out to go potty immediately. This will help you to watch your puppy and know when to take him outside to have him relieve himself. (These are not the only potty breaks you will need to housebreak your puppy, but it will put you in the right direction to housebreaking him in the long run).

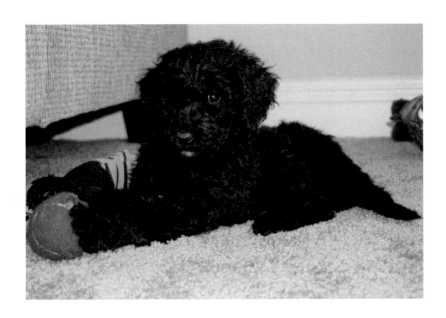

5 WHAT FOOD TO BUY YOUR PUPPY

We choose our food based on what is in it. We like to feed our puppies a food that has high protein content. You can find this information on the bag / can of food you are purchasing. There are many good brands of puppy food and many that are not as good. The way I choose a brand is not from commercials or popularity. I simply look at the 1st ingredient on the bag. I believe the first ingredient should be meat (not a meat by-product or meat "meal"). Once I find a good meat source in the food, I do check the protein content. My personal dogs seem to do better on a no grain diet – so lastly for me, I make sure the brand I use is grain free. That is not necessary for every dog. It is in my own opinion that it is best for my personal dogs.

Every puppy can react differently to different foods. The food your neighbor's puppy eats might work fantastic for that puppy, but yours might not like it or may have a different reaction to the ingredients. If you notice your puppy having soft stool for a long period of time and / or itching frequently and the vet has ruled out medical reasons, think of the food you are feeding the puppy. The food can cause simple irritations to a puppy's stomach just as it can do to us. Maybe switch from one main ingredient to another (example: chicken to lamb). Puppies can have food allergies to different ingredients which can cause an upset stomach or unwanted itching. It can be as easy as the main ingredient or much more difficult. Sometimes you need to try multiple types and flavors of food to find the one right for your puppy. Be patient and take your time to find the right diet for your puppy.

6 PUTTING YOUR PUPPY TO BED

Usually, the first night home with your new puppy is the hardest. The puppy is going to be given a new routine and expected to follow some guidelines in his new house. First of all, remember this is a stressful time for the puppy as well and he is doing the best he can do. Sometimes, it helps to exhaust the little puppy before bed. At this age, still too young to go outside for a walk or run, play with him in the house. Run with him from wall to wall or up and down the hall way. It will not take long for your cute little fur ball to get tired and start watching you instead of playing with you. At this point, your puppy is tired and ready to lie down. Take him out to go potty one last time before putting him into a crate. Make sure this potty break is not a play date outside. This is all business (potty business). Stay outside until your puppy goes potty and then reward your puppy with positive reinforcement for going in the area you have just asked him to go. Do this immediately before bed, so when you are finished, you walk inside and place your puppy into the crate for a good night's rest.

In my opinion, crate training is the fastest and easiest way to house break a puppy. At night, put the puppy in a crate to sleep. Your crate should be big enough to fit the puppy when he is grown to his full size. Use the divider that comes with the crate to make the puppy's area smaller for while he is still a puppy. The crate size given to your puppy will grow with the size of your puppy. (If you choose not to use the divider and the crate is much larger compared to your puppy size, your puppy could use half the space for a potty area while still having half the area for a sleeping area; Thus defeating the purpose of the crate.) Put a bed, blanket or towel in the crate for your puppy (along with the towel that carries mom or siblings scent if you have it). There is no harm in putting a toy or two in the crate with your puppy if you desire; however, do NOT put food or water in the crate. You cannot expect the puppy to try to make it through the night without having a potty accident if you are allowing him to eat and drink throughout the night.

Once the puppy is placed in his crate, turn off the lights and put yourself to bed. The puppy may start to whine or bark from inside the crate. Remember, the puppy has probably never been alone at night up until this night and usually has not ever had to sleep in a crate. So allow an adjustment period prior to getting too frustrated. This is where the training can be tricky. You MUST be consistent. Do not allow your puppy to be removed from the crate for barking or whining. You have a decision to make. Let the puppy cry himself to sleep, or get up, slightly punish the puppy for barking (you can use a squirt bottle of water to spray at them or a loud jar of pennies to shake at the puppy for this behavior), and go right back to bed. Do not give the puppy any positive reinforcement for making you come back out to where he is for barking. One thing new owners like to do is console their new puppy. The sweet whispers of "you're going to be ok" and "mommy loves you" are sweet, but counterproductive in this stage of training. The puppies (and dogs for that matter) love to be spoken softly to. They listen to your tone and thrive when they feel the love come from it... So if barking from their crate gets their new owner to come out and speak softly to them, then that is just what they will continue to do. So be strong and consistent. The good news about this is, if done correctly, your puppy will not only have learned a new routine but you will have formed a better bond with your puppy while keeping the role as "boss" or "top dog" in your home.

Now, the location of where to put the crate for night time sleeping is up to the new owners. Some people have the crate in their bedroom, some the living room and some even do the garage. The way I decide, is to ask myself where I want my puppy to sleep when the puppy is a bit older (whether he is still sleeping in a crate or old enough to sleep without one). If I want my puppy to grow up and always be in my bedroom, I will go ahead and start him in a crate in my bedroom. If I want the puppy to grow up and patrol the house and sleep in the living room at night, then that is where I would decide to start the crate training. There is no wrong answer to where to place the crate. It is simply a matter of opinion. You will still follow the same rules and guidelines in crate training, no matter where the crate is placed.

If you do not want to use a crate to train your puppy, there are other ways. Depending on your availability to be home with the puppy will determine the speed of success. I would still recommend limiting the space your puppy has at night time and during the day when you are not there to watch the puppy. (Maybe use a baby gate to gate off the kitchen for him or gate the doorway to a large laundry room). During the day, not only is it easier to house break a puppy that has space limited, it also helps to protect the puppy from harmful, household products and to protect your household furniture from destruction. At night time, follow the same instructions given for the puppies prior to being put into a crate. After the potty break outside, instead of placing your puppy in your crate, you would be placing him in his designated sleeping area (still with no water and no food). The goal is for the puppy to learn how to hold his potty until his new owners take him outside to the "potty area".

The next morning, I know you are going to want to get up, go to the bathroom yourself and get a nice hot cup of coffee (or tea). Instead, it would be a good idea to immediately go to the crate your puppy is in, pick the puppy up out of his crate, and carry him to the potty area you have designated for him to go potty. I say "carry" your puppy because if you don't, there is a good chance that the second you open the crate door and ask your puppy to walk out, he is going to pee. They are not yet old enough, nor have they had the routine long enough, to make it to your outside potty area without help. Once you place the puppy in his potty area, stay right there with him and watch him go potty. Immediate positive reinforcement is necessary. You placed him down on the ground expecting him to go potty and he did. Make it known to him that his behavior was appreciated and rewarded. Now you can go potty yourself and have your coffee.

7 YOUR PUPPY'S FIRST VET VISIT

Your first vet visit is an important one. Most breeders ask you to go to your vet for a health checkup within 48 hours of bringing the puppy home. They do this to protect you, the new owner, and them, the breeder. The breeder should be sending you home with an active, healthy puppy. The vet visit is for your vet to acknowledge that the breeder has done a good job and has provided you with a healthy puppy. Although this is a wise thing to do, you must be careful. If your new puppy is between 8 and 10 weeks old when you bring him home, your puppy is not fully vaccinated. Which means your puppy is susceptible to all kinds of disease in the world, especially at a vet's office. So, when you bring your new puppy to his first vet visit, it is important to protect him. Bring a large towel and hold your puppy in the towel in the waiting room. Do NOT let that puppy touch the floor of the vet they visit. Remember, as clean as the vet offices try to be, there is always a chance that your puppy can walk on something that was contaminated with a virus or a disease. It is a vet office and they do treat sick animals. So to be extra careful, the puppy does not walk on or touch the floor of the vet office while you visit. I would also limit the amount of attention the puppy gets from strangers in the vet office. As cute as your puppy is, I am sure there will be a lot of people wanting to say hello to your new addition. Unfortunately, that is just another way your puppy can get sick. You do not know where their animal has been or why they are at the vet's office. (Is there dog sick? Carrying germs?) So it would be best to educate people on how easily a puppy can get sick and how you would prefer nobody pet your puppy while in the waiting room. Some people take offense to this and I am sorry that they do. As you enter the exam room, the same rule applies. Do NOT put your puppy directly on the exam table. First, spread the towel you brought from your home on the exam table and then place your puppy on your towel. Your vet will completely understand why you have chosen to do this and will not have a problem with it at all. After you get a full exam, pick your puppy up in the towel and continue to keep him off any floors or counters until you arrive safely back to your home. By following these directions, you are limiting your puppy's exposure to disease that can severely harm him quickly. When it comes to a loved family companion, it is better to be safe than to be sorry.

8 GROOMING

Grooming can be as easy as giving your puppy a bath once a month, to as complicated as weekly baths, hair trims, ear cleanings and daily brushes. Depending on the breed of dog you have, your level of difficulty changes. Short haired dogs who have fur (not hair) can usually get away with having a bath when needed (ie dog smells, dog gets bath). The longer the hair, usually the more grooming is required. The non – shedding breeds that have hair (not fur) usually require daily brushings and hair trims or cuts every few weeks. The one thing I really like to do when grooming is to clean my dog's ears with a cleansing solution I buy at the pet store. I like to clean my dog's ears weekly as a preventative to them getting ear infections. This is not because they have had a bad history of infections; I do this because it makes me feel more confident on being proactive about something that can sometimes be preventable.

Grooming a puppy is important. You want to get the puppy used to being groomed while he is still young, so that the puppy does not grow to fear the groomer. There are loud noises (blow dryer) and tools they do not see on a daily basis. The groomer will be touching every part of the puppy's body and moving the puppy's body to get a good angle for their grooming. If you can, I would introduce your puppy to these items (blow dryer, scissors, faucets) in your home and I would practice playing with their paws, legs and tails until your puppy is old enough to have all his shots. This is a great exercise not only to get your puppy used to being touched everywhere by a groomer, but also to prepare your puppy to behave around young children who like to touch. Again, the puppy's immune system is not as strong as it needs to be to encounter some of the germs that can be brought into a grooming parlor or mobile grooming van. This does not mean that the groomer has a dirty store. It means that your puppy is simply too young to be out in public with the variety of animals that go in and out of their stores. Once your puppy is fully vaccinated, you should not need to worry about taking your pet to a grooming parlor or having a groomer come to you.

9 TRAINING

Consistency is key to training your new puppy. Everyone in the house hold, including children old enough to understand, must be on the same page. The punishments should be the same, the corrections should be the same and the reward should be the same. Your puppy should NEVER get away with bad behavior. Like children, they crave discipline and live happier lives when taught to behave in an appropriate manner. And just for the record, puppies are never too young to learn!

Chewing

Your puppy is going to have a need to chew. If not given the appropriate chew toys to sink his teeth into, he will chew on different things throughout the house that he can find to chew. This would include baseboards, furniture, shoes, sandals and anything else accessible. Every puppy likes different toys; however I like to give them a bit of a variety. Maybe a small plush animal or bone, a rubber tire on a rope has always been a favorite, and multiple small toys they can carry around with them. I recommend having a couple toys in every area you allow your puppy to be in. So if you are going to let him be in the living room with you while you watch TV, make sure to have a couple toys in the living room that he has access to chew on, while he is in that room. The same goes for any other room that you will allow your puppy to be in. When the puppy is put in his crate, or the designated puppy area for when you are not home, go ahead and put a couple good toys in with him. That way the puppy has an opportunity to entertain himself while he is alone.

House training

Bringing home a puppy is so much fun! The playing, the cuddling, the puppy smells... All so cute! The one not so fun chore that comes with bringing a puppy home (besides pooper scooping the backyard) is the house breaking! The speed at which you master this chore is based upon the work you do as the owner. As with everything else in this book, consistency is key to raising a puppy!

I use the crate training method myself. The crate, when used correctly, is an amazing tool. It is not supposed to be used as your puppy's living space. It is a training tool designed to help owners train the puppies to grow into happy, healthy, adult dogs. The crate is a safe space for your puppy to go when you are not home to keep your puppy safe or at night when you are asleep and unable to monitor puppy.

Here is how to use a crate correctly. Allow your puppy immediately to walk in and out of the crate with the door open. You can leave bedding in the crate (and possibly the towel you brought home from the breeder's house that has mom's or sibling's scent on it). Your puppy should be able to freely go in and out of the crate at his discretion. When a time comes where you are unable to monitor your puppy (while you are in the shower or going to the grocery store), put your puppy into the crate and lock the door. It is important to take your puppy outside to go potty in his designated potty area before placing the puppy into the crate. This will help him to not have an accident in the crate, as the puppy is not going to be used to having to hold his potty. The puppy will stay in the crate while you shower and get ready for your day. When finished, pick the puppy up and out of the crate and carry him to the designated potty area. Remain there until he goes potty. Any time you are taking him outside to specifically go potty, you need to remain calm and don't start any puppy playing games until the business is done. Once he goes potty, you can give him praise and begin a game. The next time you are unable to monitor the puppy, you would repeat those steps. Go potty, praise the puppy, put the puppy in his crate, leave, come back and carry the puppy out to his potty area and praise the puppy again. As I said in an earlier chapter, the reason why you carry your puppy to the designated potty area instead of allowing him to follow you out by walking is because of the chance of the puppy having an accident between the crate and the potty area. As the puppy gets older and learns his routine, the puppy will know where he is going from the crate and he will automatically walk to the potty area. Just takes time to learn.

Now, during the beginning stages of crate training, it is not uncommon for the puppy to have a couple accidents in his crate. Don't get frustrated. The puppy is just as upset by this as you are and that will help the puppy to learn that he does not want to go potty inside the crate because then he is stuck in there with it. Usually, this only happens a couple times before the puppy is able to understand that if he waits, his owners will come get him and take him out to the potty area where he is allowed to go potty.

Housebreaking without using a crate can be a bit trickier, but certainly doable. I do still believe it is in yours and your puppy's best interest to keep his space limited when you are not there to monitor him. Use a baby gate or two to keep the puppy in the kitchen area where there is a tile floor instead of carpet. This would be helpful because the puppy is still in training and you need to expect some accidents while you are gone.

When you are home with the puppy, you need to monitor the puppy the best you can. The second you see the puppy sniff around the floor (sometimes they will start to walk in a circle), get up and grab the puppy. Carry the puppy outside to the designated potty area quickly and wait for the puppy to continue to look for a spot to go potty. Again, this is not play time outside. This is all about going potty. Once the puppy goes potty, give him positive reinforcement and bring the puppy back inside to play. If the puppy has an accident in front of you, you do need to punish him. Take the puppy and show the puppy the spot, hold him there and clap your hands real loud to scare the puppy. You want the puppy to associate the potty accident with something bad. I also say

"No!" Once you punish the puppy, you take the puppy outside to the designated potty area. If possible, wait to see if the puppy needs to go potty again so you can finish on a positive reinforcement. If not, that is ok. You were still able to show the puppy the behavior he did was unacceptable and where the appropriate place for him to go potty is.

A lot of people like to put the puppy outside when they are at work so that the puppy is unable to have an accident in the house. There isn't anything wrong with that as long as you live in an area where the weather permits it and there are no wild animals that could grab your puppy while you are gone (remember, a coyote can easily scale a 6 foot fence with your puppy in his mouth). However, this does not help to potty train your puppy. You are not asking your puppy to learn how to hold his bladder while you are at work if the puppy is outside. The puppy simply has the freedom to go when and where he wants to, in the boundaries that he was given. So as much as it is easier, usually it makes the house training harder because all the time outside is time without "practice".

Commands

It is never too early to start to train your puppy at home. I say "at home" because until your puppy has completed all of his puppy vaccinations to keep him safe in public, he really should just stay in the safety of your home.

The command "sit" is usually a good command to start with. I like to train my dogs to sit for their food when it is feeding time. Once they sit, I reward them by giving them their food in their bowls. There are many different training techniques used by trainers. To train my puppies to sit, I use a reward system;

however instead of using treats (they have the potential to be too rich for a younger puppy under the age of 3 or 4 months), I use their puppy kibble. I take a handful and throw it in a bag that I can place in my pocket. I take one piece of kibble at a time and I say the word "sit" as I use the kibble to guide my puppy's head up over his own body. By doing this, they naturally want to sit so they can look up naturally. As soon as their bottom hits the floor, I say "good sit", reward with the treat and then continue to reward with positive reinforcement (tons of petting and rubbing). Now, as I am rewarding the puppy, he has already given up his sit position. That is ok. This is the beginning to the puppy understanding the command. As time goes on, they will sit for a longer period of time, on your command. Be patient and be consistent.

Another good command that we like to use is "off". Our dogs are part of our family; however, we have furniture the dogs know that they are not allowed to be on. The way we trained the command "off" was to gently grab their collar and pull them off the piece of furniture, while saying the word "off". As soon as their body was off the furniture, we would praise them with positive reinforcement. On top of learning "off", we would also use the voice sound of "eh, eh" anytime they looked like they were going to try and get on that piece of furniture again. We wanted them to know that the piece of furniture they were trying to jump on was off limits. This only works if everyone in the household is consistent with the same rules. They either are or are not allowed on that piece of furniture. It does not mean they cannot get on any furniture... just the designated pieces you have decided to keep them off. Our dogs know they are allowed in our beds in our home, however they are not allowed on either of our couches. This is another command we start immediately after bringing a puppy home.

There are a lot of different commands you can teach your puppy as he grows into a well behaved dog. I always recommend training, but I do not believe you have to hire a trainer to accomplish it. Training can be done in the comfort of your home as long as you are consistent and reward the appropriate behavior. In my opinion, the most important commands to master with your new puppy are "sit" and "stay". This can come in handy when something goes wrong at home or in public and you quickly just need your dog to be still for the time given.

Training is more than just commands. Bad behavior needs to be addressed and corrected immediately. A common problem new owners have with puppy behavior is when the puppy tries to use his teeth to grab onto the pant legs of the owners, or more commonly, the children. This can cause children to scream and accidental scratches and bite marks on the heels of the person wearing the pants in question. This is VERY common so please don't panic or think your puppy has aggressive behavior. Take your time to stop and correct the behavior every time it starts. In my experience, the best way to correct this behavior is to grab the puppy and place your thumb under the puppy's tongue and apply some pressure. The puppy is not going to like this correction at all. He will squirm and might even whine; however, you need to be consistent and hold your ground for 3 – 5 seconds. While your thumb is in the puppy's mouth, firmly say "No!" Then place the puppy back on the ground and continue with whatever you were doing prior to the incident. There is a good chance the puppy is going to grab at the pant legs again. No problem. Calmly grab the puppy, place your thumb under his tongue again and apply the pressure. Do all this while again saying "No!" The puppy will quickly learn that every time he places his mouth on those desirable pant legs, he gets the undesirable thumb in his mouth.

Once understood, the behavior will stop. The hardest part to this method is teaching the kids how to do it gently, yet firmly. Puppies are smart enough to understand who will punish and who will not. So everyone in the household needs to understand the punishment is necessary and needs to be done every time the puppy grabs their clothes. I use this technique any time my puppy puts something in his mouth that is not allowed, including chewing on my fingers or other body parts. Chewing is for chew toys ONLY! Be consistent.

As far as training goes, there are many different commands and tricks your puppy can learn. Go slowly and be patient. I usually allow my dog to conquer 1 trick per week when training. That way, even if he has mastered the trick in the first day, the puppy gets 6 more days of positive reinforcement on that trick, making training not only fun, but rewarding. If you are not interested in training your puppy fun tricks, training is still very much needed. Never let your puppy get away with unwanted behavior. This can include barking, jumping, running out the door, among other things. Set the rules and boundaries the day the puppy steps foot into your home. It is much easier to set the boundaries now, then to allow bad behavior in the beginning and to have to start from "square one" after the bad behaviors have been formed and allowed.

10 SOCIALIZING

A common concern among new puppy owners is how to raise a socialized puppy when the puppy is too young to have all his puppy shots. It is not safe to go to dog parks, dog beaches, puppy training classes or any other popular dog hang outs until your puppy has had all the vaccinations needed for his first year of life. At an average, the puppy is about 4 month old when they reach this point. So how do you make sure the puppy remains friendly with other dogs in a single - dog household? In my opinion, waiting until the puppy is 4 months old and fully vaccinated before playing with any other dogs will not hurt his future social skills. However, I understand the concern and the want to have your puppy raised with other dogs. In this case, the only thing I would do (so your puppy still stays safe from disease) is allow one or 2 dogs owned by family or close friends to visit. These dogs

MUST be current on all vaccinations weeks prior to meeting your new puppy. They also must not be allowed to go to high traffic dog areas at least 2 weeks prior to meeting the new puppy. The visiting dog is going to go through a quarantine period to prevent him from bringing in anything harmful to your puppy. This means the owner of the visiting dog must be okay with not visiting the dog parks, beaches, pet stores or going for walks in public with their dog. They also must agree to give their dog a good bath, making sure to scrub the bottom of the dog's feet thoroughly before bringing the dog into your home to visit with your puppy. (Remember, an older vaccinated dog can carry disease on their paws without showing symptoms of having the disease themselves). If you have a family member or good friend that you can trust to take all the necessary precautions when allowing their dog to play with your new puppy, then it is in my opinion that your puppy would remain safe. However, if it were my puppy that I was raising in my home, I would simply wait until my puppy was old enough to be fully vaccinated prior to arranging play dates with other dogs.

Once your dog is fully vaccinated (around 4 months of age), then it is safe to go for walks in public and arrange play dates with other dogs. I do recommend taking your puppy into public and / or around your friend's dogs both to socialize your puppy and to expose your puppy to new sounds, smells and experiences. Just like children, puppies need experiences to become well rounded. The more sounds and smells your puppy gets accustomed to, the easier it will be for him to adjust on new adventures.

This is about the time I would start to teach my puppy how to ride safely in the car. Start with short trips... around the block maybe. Praise your puppy when he first gets into the car and talk calmly to your puppy as you drive. Use words like "good boy" to show that whatever he is doing, you like it, which in turn, pleases the puppy. If you are going to expect your puppy (when full grown) to wear a harness made to hook up to a seatbelt, introduce it now. As your puppy starts to be comfortable in the car on your short journeys, start taking him on longer ones. Go to a friend's house or visit with family. Make the car ride an enjoyable feature for your puppy. Have the outcome be positive (this can be as simple as stopping at a friend's house where they will shower your puppy with loads of attention). The idea of this exercise is not only to get your puppy able to ride in a car without getting car sick, but to also show him that not every car ride ends at the vet hospital. Although some will, most of them will end in a positive manner, allowing the dog to want to go for a ride rather than dread it.

Now your puppy is old enough to enjoy the world with you. He is safe from disease and has turned into a healthy, happy, well socialized young adult. You can now enjoy all the fun activities that your city has for people to bring their pets. Check out local hikes, dog beaches and pet friendly restaurants where you are allowed to sit and enjoy the view outside with your companion by your side.

Having a dog is such a rewarding experience and the bond you build through the years only grows stronger by the day. You will find that not only are you providing love for your dog, but your dog will provide some much needed support for you in times of need.

ABOUT THE AUTHOR

Leslie Oakley lives in Menifee, California with her fiancé Dave, her step son David, and her daughter Kylie. She was born with a love for animals and has spent her life as an adult fulfilling her need to be surrounded by the creatures she adores. She is a reputable dog breeder and prides herself on the care and love she gives each of her animals, including her beloved Miniature Pot Bellied Pig, Bobbie. Along with dogs, puppies and a pig, Leslie and her family also own chickens and hope to bring a couple horses home someday. Leslie plans to write more books to help people understand and connect with their animals, as she believes that people can build a much better bond with their pets if they learn to understand them and their needs.

Made in the USA
San Bernardino, CA
28 June 2020